T0113804

Blot On The Landscape
Poems

John Ngong Kum Ngong

Langaa Research & Publishing CIG
Mankon, Bamenda

Publisher:
Langaa RPCIG
Langaa Research & Publishing Common Initiative Group
P.O. Box 902 Mankon
Bamenda
North West Region
Cameroon
Langaagrp@gmail.com
www.langaa-rpcig.net

Distributed in and outside N. America by African Books Collective
orders@africanbookscollective.com
www.africanbookscollective.com

ISBN: 9956-792-22-5

DISCLAIMER
All views expressed in this publication are those of the author and do
not necessarily reflect the views of Langaa RPCIG.

Table of Contents

If You Were Human

Seasons, if you were human,
understanding and forthright
as you roll across the world,
if you could communicate
I would put forward my case
for fairness and equity.
I would beg you to give me
the prerogative to choose
the time and the location,
the shoes and the ensemble
to put on day after day
and the place to place my head
as you glide across the globe
gracing or soiling the earth.

I know that you can never
overturn the status quo
nor stand up to your master
but you can be less severe
as you visit the whole world.
The heart of the dry season
and that of the rainy span
if pressed to Nature's large breasts
would, come hell or high water
satisfy my strange longing
to burn blot on the landscape.
It takes all the strength in me
to turn the key on anger
when floods devastate our homes
and bush fires fell forests.

If you were somehow human
I would prepare you hemlock.

Seasons, if you could arbitrate,
a green carpet will bejewel
the bumpy surface of my land,
many fruit trees will be in bud
and the scent of life will mushroom
during the dripping cold season.
The sun clement will feed them well
till harvest appropriates their souls
and man gathers for survival.
If you could imprison my thoughts,
nurse through the measles in my blood
and deliver up your whip hand
I would turn towards the full moon
unclothed, unshaven and unkempt
to retrieve my mental balance.
If you were a human being
I would hammer you upside down
and blot out blot on the landscape.

Eco Sworn Enemies

I remember G.R.A.*
Buea, once so green and clean
now so brown and repulsive
thick with unsavoury smells
and infectious diseases.

The green hedges of yesteryear
and the carpet grass her treasure
have been swept away not by floods
but by eco sworn enemies
draining the earth of gracefulness.

The beautifully trimmed lawns,
the gardens and their flowers
that made me beam like a child
each time I visited them
are now blots on the landscape.

I burn for a new G.R.A.
not exclusively in Buea.
l burn for it in the nation
for greenery to protect us
from an ecological stroke.

*G.R.A. Government Residential Area.

The Garbage Bags Are Full

The garbage bags by you
are full to the fringes.
The smell of dead livestock
drives the rich to wear masks.
Death dawdles here and there
hoping to smile once more.

We wake up everyday
blank and mute as tombstones
not able to move through
the dung of decadence.
Owls hoot from our rooftops
and pus drips from our eyes.

You nourish feathered friends
without wings in your heart.
The claws of stern History
deep in our psyche mushroom.
Foxes wait for pickings
and sharks look for fresh hearts.

The garbage bags are full
and crows sing above us,
their beaks red with booty.
The dirt and filth of fear
thrash us through thin and thick
thinning down our thin lives
lingering in the cold
at the edge of collapse.

Death Waits in the Wings

The smell of urine
needles your nostrils
early in the morning
as you wind your way
through dung-coloured huts
on your way to work.

The sick city wakes
with mist in her eyes.
Somewhere a brown mouse shrieks
and scares a cockroach
about to breakfast
on human faeces.

The sun rises slowly,
creeps across the pale sky
and then clenches its hot fists
to strike the head of earth.
In agony of mind
thousands fall in the dust.

Look into your sore hearts
for the silt and the slime
left to lay waste the mind.
In the heart of our shame
a crow upturns a can
teeming with sleek maggots.
The liquid putrescence
streaming down your backyard
soaks into the cracked walls

of neighbours without means.
The stomach-turning smell
compels the lungs to scream.

Blind death waits in the wings
sure of seasoned supplies
where sewage churns out blue flies.
The wrinkled face of Love
with fresh wounds in her heart
moans in our mud and muck.

Breathing with Difficulty

Breathing with difficulty
in the tight embrace of dung
the spokesman of dirty dogs
lies silent in his vomit.
He believes the stench of death
and the worms in his nostrils
will have nothing but praise for
his bulldog guts and hunger
for the eyes of rotten bulls.

If the mouthpiece of carrion
looks carefully around him
with the eyes of a Romeo
he will see the land in waste
and feel the itch of decay.
He will kick the arse of dirt
and vomit the grains of shame
that have made of this country
a hell for those who hate filth.

We live where refuse is wine
in the heart of the nation
where mucus and afterbirth
are as fresh as a daisy.
You always flash a broad smile
willing to have fun on dung
like maggots in a dead dog.
Your breath is a stinking pot
full of rank mutton and beef.

These many years of lean life
have done nothing to change you.
The same putrid train of thought
not cut out for giving rise
to beauty that clears the mind
remains grubby in your blood.
We are a people from the hills
used to gulping taintless air
with see-through minds and warm hearts.

A Stroll with My Me

I take a stroll with my me
down a street oozing mucus
at the height of a hot day.
All the flies rush towards me
grumbling and shaking their fists.
They think I am intruding.

I take to my heels briskly
my throat almost constricting
but the stench hangs on like death.
My spent heart comes round gently
as the sun begins to die
against hills bereft of trees.

The flies return to their banquet
chatting, bewildered by my flight.
I sit down on a worn-out slab
to let my aching me vomit
the plateful of putrefaction
I pressurised him to swallow.

Evening creeps in quietly
in a purple evening gown.
My me upset wants us to leave.
I take a different route back home,
a breeding ground for cholera
in the marrow of the city.

Tall But Bare

The slim slippery streets
strewn with rotting garbage
steam with rotten apples
bent on blowing to bits
those who stand up to them
or break into their zone.

The foul smell reminds me
how my mum trod the streets
cleaning dustbins and rot,
stinking of beer and slime
near whitewashed waveless tombs.
She dumped me here one day
bored with her dish of pain.

I have grown tall but bare
and bear my plight with care
walking down the same streets
without my brave mother.
My life is now a storm,
my thirst for glow my pain.
I live but am not seen,
I dream but kiss dead wood.

My life is but cracked hands
my ache for self my death
without bloom without tears.
Alone like an outcast
I bemoan my doomed fate
amidst dustbins and rot

near dead leaves and dead fields.
The woodlands are all gone
and my ozone sheet torn.

Thick smoke from breweries,
chemicals from factories
and frequent oil spillage
have rent our blue blanket.
Pollution everywhere
has knocked holes in the lungs
of the ozone layer
our last hope of living.
Why must my life be dung
because of my birthplace?

Aberration

In the filth of our thoughts
we master the maiming
and the poisoning too
of evey mind that thinks
above the heights we climb.

Sometimes we do not hesitate
to kill everything that is green
to spread our filthy feelings on.
We cover long long distances
looking for forests to despoil
for our empires to flourish.

We mangle many sincere tongues
to stem the tide of a revolt
and crush the balls of agitprops.
We are vicious and venomous
and build our homes by injustice.
You think it is humiliating
to live on your own waste matter.

Often we drink our own urine
to penetrate deep into you
day after day to enjoy life
building the way we desire
wherever whenever we want.
Leave us a place in your bosom,
an apartment where we can change
when we wish to wreck without noise.

Sick City

The fresh fish roasting smelt nice.
The sun had just retreated
and darkness dressed in charcoal
began to veil the landscape.
The woman roasting the fish
sang a song ,a gripping song,
a song about two children
scrubbing latrines and kitchens
to thrive in this sick city
where honesty and merit
have been thrown out like foul water.
It is hard not to remember
the dearth of trees and greenery
in this drab dog eat dog city.

The woman's song shook my heart
as pear trees in an orchard
shake in a gust of dry wind.
I found myself before her
eager despite the rank smell
of urine and rotting flesh
to listen to her sweet song.
The smell of the fish trapped me.
I felt empty inside me
like a pumpkin without seeds
then a longing to vamoose
from the foul place arrested me.
I think now is the time to tame
the tongues that butcher greenery.

Overpowered by hunger
I bought a good chunk of fish,
sat down near three ghostlike folk
who kept saying that rulers
like all proud people will fall
and their roots will waste away.
Their tongues were sharpened machetes
and their target, learned men
lost in political pranks
stinking the place out with booze.
I left my fish uneaten
hungry to quit this sick city
to where hummingbirds make merry
and the lives of trees not taken.

Blot on the Landscape

Our forefathers were straightforward,
they said what they saw and esteemed.
They held each other's hand in love
and kept their environment clean.

They stayed together like a rock,
they opened the soil and sowed seed.
They experienced their ups and downs
but sang songs soaked in sobriety.

Today their songs are still wholesome
ringing in my ears like new bells.
Their love still surges in my veins
raging against high-handed gods
shipping our cocoa and timber,
the treasure of our land for free.
Our forefathers were straightforward.
Why can we not behave like them?

Our forefathers were straightforward,
they opened their hearts to sleep well
and kept their doors open to all.
We delight in dipping others
in pots of scalding hot water
to kiss the cunt of a warthog
in the height of the dry season
to proclaim plenty from lecterns.

You are a blot on the landscape
dead wood in the grip of a bull
determined to have a breakthrough
in and out of the arena.
Like a partridge that hatches eggs
it made no effort to produce,
the bull romps home by unjust means
resolved to shoot without missing.
Seasons breeze in and fizzle out
but you stay put like a donkey
refusing to rush or turn tail
fallen for the stool on the landscape.

Desert Heat

In the desert heat
of this plastic place
the wind weeps daily
heavy with thick smoke
from whale breweries
in the eye of town
blot on the landscape.

Respectable folk sing
the excesses of greed,
the deceit and the dirt,
the bitches and the base
we refuse to embrace
even in dark corners
blotting out our breeding.

In the Sahara heat
of this knotty country
self has grown carbuncles
dripping wet with chagrin.
My hair is falling off
as if beriberi
has built in my system
holding out against blot.

The beetle's hum is gone,
the strains of the ear stalled
in this bloodthirsty heat
determined to stay on.
Moles no longer come out

and dragon flies have fled
to where water whispers
and the wind flogs the eyes.

Sore Mother

The earth my sore mother
is thirsty for a stroke
and a kiss from the rain.
The air dry as a bone
boxes the ears of hope
with phalanges of flint
in the heart of bald fields
waiting to be bedecked
in assorted colours
when the rain breaks the drought.

The clouds have taken flight,
the sky arrayed in blue
looks down in bulging pride
the brown cracking visage
of my anguished mother
parched and weary of hoes.
The drought has robbed my mum
of her joy and sparkle
this season of dryness
fraught with pain and scurvy.
Hungering mouths struck dumb
die in the dust of shame.

Intense heat imprisons beetles
in the underbelly of earth
and praying mantis shy away.
Crickets fear jumping and dancing
into piping hot nights their time.
Owls in their numbers fly out though

with their grating signature tunes
tearing the spirit of the drive
to brave another dry season
even when overwhelming dust
barges in without permission.
Let this prolonged baking spell break
before my white garment is burnt
for the land to breathe normally.

Realm of Dust

In every field dust
morning noon and night.
Dust in our reason
dust on our profiles
dust in our manners
dust in our dwellings
dust on our bodies
dust in our dealings
dust even in death
dust in the system
dust in your workshop
dust in our voices
dust in the dry love
we fling at neighbours
when the sun sips us
in this realm of dust.

The thin on the ground
grass that once was here
has gone up in flames.
The air is torrid
replete with fart
and the smell of death.
Children cannot play
in this realm of dust
so hot and so fierce.
The land is naked,
the trees caked with blot
and every stream dead.
Animals and men

crawl long like lizards
for a day's ration
in this realm of dust.
My heart is a blaze
in this cloud of dust.

I see crows athirst
on the breasts of dames
daft to let their milk
flow without a fee.
The blood on their laps
reminds me of vamps,
torture and abuse.
I try not to think
but my skin tingles
not with excitement
like a would be bride
but with cringing fear
like a raped virgin.
My heart in on coals
burning in the sun
in this realm of dust.

Dry Season

Split lips bleeding
in grit and grime.
Cracked soles sobbing
in bleak and blot
spent in the dust.
It is the dry season.

The sun drunk with power
strikes at the heart of grief
content with the season.
The dust pregnant with scorn
hunts most often the eye.
It is the dry season.

The wind screaming
waking from sleep
wraps its steel arms
round the spare necks
of souls near death.
It is their dry season.

The prima donna here
gargantuan corrupt flesh
does not acknowledge you
nor the vermilion tears
burning your toasted cheeks.
It is your dry season.
What once was green
this spring of strains
brimming with life

now lies wrung out
dry as a bone.
It is our dry season.

Livestock and dogs drop dead
in sun-baked villages.
Savage beasts keel over
crumple and come to dust
in the measureless wild.
It is their dry season.

I feel guilty
watching my kind
tumble and rot.
The shame of it
claws and clubs me.
It is my dry season.

Everyman here and there
twitches and passes out.
Petty tyrants are dumb,
they know no dry season.
The state is deaf and dumb,
the dry season stays on.

Weary Of Life

Faint and weary of life
the yellow leaf sighed twice
detached itself pain-free
from the uppermost branch
and floated down from the tree
gently till it kissed the earth.
The branch that had shouldered it
whispered a sigh of relief.

Like a bolt from the blue
a sweeping gust of wind
swept through where I squatted
whisking the leaf elsewhere.
The earth moaned and groaned distraught
as the wind tore through the zone
breaking the arms of weak trees
and taking apart botched roofs.

Thrown off balance I rose,
looked at the brown landscape
and the blank stones hard by
cutting me down to size.
Three dozen and three years now
I have tried without success
to cart off like the fierce wind
the wear and tear at your door.

Watching the Last Leaves

I watch with dismay
the last yellow leaves
fall from the pear trees
we grew up to love.
Before we kissed them
others had done so
to feed their households
and renew their blood.

I watch with distress
the last soothing leaves
fall from these pear trees.
I can neither weep
nor stop their demise.
Their loss triggers heat
and gives birth to tears
in a world of sores.

The loss is a thorn,
it pierces the minds
that roam around it
mute and scared to death.
Dog days will kill us
unless we stand up
against both blue funk
and the bloody beasts
tearing our hearts out
for more leaves to fall.

Our seeds need shelter
to shoot up blooming
even on hard soil
or on rocky ground.
We need to back them
even when our flesh
and our trunks are spent
to dodge the munching
of our own sweepings
and plant new pear trees.

Looking For New Terrain

Green life thrives here no more
since bird-brains killed the grass
and cut down the fruit trees
that gave us cause to live
even when fields were bleak
and bulls wanted fresh blood.

No more sparkling sparrows,
no more swanking swallows
this way to sing us green
or listen to our sobs
under the knife edge heat
and the bulls' hatchet men.

Grasshoppers cry daily
behind high and dry leaves.
The Saharan air laughs
and brooding bottleflies
hover over my crown,
much in the dead of night.

The dreams I entertained,
virescent dreams at youth
roam naked through the land
like ghosts hoarse and baleful
looking for new terrain
since the bulls swept the board.

Notes of woe fill the air
and worms crawl in the day
majestic and happy
in the realm of the bulls.
Weary of time and heat
the rose bows to the worms.

Intellectuals for fear
reign in their offices
coated with sheets of grime.
The land limps exhausted
ravaged by bloody bulls
blot on this rare landscape.

Gone the Green of Yesterday

We fetched fresh water here
in and out of season
at dawn in years gone by
conscious of the canker
that could burst forth and spread,
wiping out countless souls
if we emptied our bowels there
or dumped carcasses in the stream.

We fetched cooling water
at twilight from the stream
whistling heartening tunes
before modern brains came
and the monster squabbling took root.
Stillbirths and unwanted babies
unseen, request a heart with claws
to tear the heart of pollution.

There are tears in the darkness
as ditched babes battle for life
in the flotsam and jetsam
encroaching the whole nation.
I am ashamed of your silence
in the face of such ugliness.
A man like you should be gutted
and trees planted to take your place.

Listen companion of crows
puffing like a bloated toad.
Listen to the deep deep drums
of the unborn beating fast

in the green of yesterday.
The sweating sky rejects mildew
and the wind cutting as a knife
vows to sunder your toneless tongue.

Paradise Lost

This place was our paradise
ever green, ever so green
teeming with bees and beetles
in conversation with ants
running up and down plum trees
glad to be free in nature.
Antelopes and porcupines
used to parade the landscape.
Sometimes lions and tigers
raced into the place hungry.

This place was ever so cute
till they came the parasites
and chose to blow to pieces
our life and our happiness.
The birds and the butterflies
that used to grace our eden
have all taken to the air
in the clutches of panic.
They have not returned since then
and the earth is very sad.

The trees in our countryside
ever green, ever so green
grew together with wild pigs
fending freely in the wild
till the parasites turned up
to kill them to fill their chests.
All the animals are dead
and the trees are felled daily.

I hold in my hand my breath
looking for leaves for my wounds.

Remember dear countrymen
gripped by the fever of wealth.
This place was our paradise
ever green, ever so green
till the lewd leeches appeared
and chose to live on our blood
to refill their treasuries
with dollars from our felled trees.
If we do not stop this trend
the desert will swallow us.

Divided

The fruit trees we planted
in the oriental part
of this perplexing state
have all grown pale and sick
stung by wasps of profit.
They will soon cease to be
not because they are old
but because the wild wasps
like white ants attacked them.

Your pestiferous tongue
like the sting of the wasps
wedges the wild attack
and perverts like mad minds
the ways of our people.
We no longer kiss age
or mind how we peg out
young and old slain by slime,
the slime in our thinking.

The evening darkens
and the earth dense with heat
vows to kill more cattle
to kill its lust for blood.
Many crops have withered
and I have seen people
drop dead in the harsh heat.
I have also caught sight
of the fat of the starved
burning with a fierce flame

but you laugh at their lot
and conceive more evil.

I feel down in the dumps
and cannot stand the smell
of burning flesh and fat.
I have watched you this long
from this side of the fence.
Cast of mind divides us
in this part of the world.
The fruits I love the best
get burnt in the mad flames
blazing in your hard heart.
Take back your name from dogs
to cheer me ere I leave.

Leaning On A Dead Trunk

Leaning on a dead trunk
on the way to my house
in the mouth of marshland
at the end of the day,
my mind always journeys.
It is often a long journey
fraught with thunderstorms and sand dunes,
a journey without grass and trees,
a journey with no drop of rain
to soften the earth for new seeds.

When my mind comes back home
I remember days of glee,
days of prestige with lightning
ready to strike defaulters.
I have nourished this image
and also preserved it jealously
in a very strong chest in my heart.
I have often walked close the image
striving always to keep it shinning,
matching it with who we ought to be.

Leaning on the dead trunk
on the way to my home
in the belly of blot
at the close of the day
reminds me of the dead
and the total breakdown in mores.
Politicians grow fat and sleek
excreting on our dignity.

It is such a sad sad story
but new seeds are under the earth.

In a couple of outbursts
the rains would come down pelting.
The earth will quench its long thirst,
the new seeds all filled with bliss
will split the hard soil and sprout.
They will all grow tall and sturdy
spreading out wide wide their branches.
I see them in my male mind's eye
bearing beautiful healthy fruits
before I bite the waiting dust.

Scared

If I could lay my me
under the mango tree
in the field in your heart
to wait and feel the wind
rustle its full branches,
I would make my bed there
to listen to the birds
sing their disappointment.

They cannot eat the fruits
even when they are ripe
and tumble to the ground.
Barbed wire in the air,
tripwire on the ground
and landmines in the heart
put a lid on their dreams.
Only fruit flies in gloom
can stand the forlonness.

If I could lay my me
in the woods in the east
and the grass in the west,
I would sail to the south
and take wing to the north
on the wings of my wit
to wine and dine bodies
ready to eat a horse.
Joy and gladness are gone
with the forests shipped out.

My mindful mind's eye and I
troubled like a restless sea
assemble time after time
to chew over the future
of our country without trees.
We have longed to emigrate
to where everything green grins
catered for like human babes
but are scared of the unknown.
If zest could be traced in you
we would urge you to grow trees.

Leave Me the Landscape

On this barren surface
in this polluted place
crawl the faint and wretched.
Crows together with owls
dine in the market square.
I feel sorry for souls
who dead from the neck up
see no good in flora.

I sing the waste the rape
of my scenic landscape
with my entire heart.
Felled trees and broken boughs
bleed the oil from my veins.
Take my paint and my brush,
take even my wallet
but leave me the landscape
deep green and natural.

I will not cease citing
the birds and the beetles,
the crickets' kissing songs,
the woodpeckers at work,
the elephants in love
walking the doomed forest
and the fields bleak and bare
even when the rains come.

Take my pen and my songs
but leave me the landscape.

Leave me the ravished landscape,
the flora and the fauna
brutalized day in day out
by hunters and lumberjacks
to keep body and soul warm.
My heart is split between them
and our scarce ecosystem
faced with total destruction.
Leave me the abused landscape
for green life to shoot once more
or cut the throat of your soul.

Pumpkins Will Flourish Again

The dry season will end someday
in this ditched part of the country
and pumpkins will flourish again
in the backyard of genuine poets.
The monster division will die
in this mean part of the nation
and wombs of sly tongues will burst
in the storm brewing close at hand.

Though your ancient grudge and contempt
hang like a millstone round my neck
even now that I have no teeth
and my children are on exile,
I turn my hand still to writing.
All day long you knock us about
and scheme to bar our kindred from
having a share in the land's fat.

The day will come when your smugness
becomes too oppressive to bear
and the air around your person
too coarse and polluted to breathe.
On that day maggots will spurn you
and the purple cords of the grave
will coil around your neck like a snake
just when you think things are okay.

I hear your people cry naked
under the weight of bereavement.
I feel like condoling with you

for my foolish heart is friendly
and I am human after all
but the smell of rot repels me.
Many more hearts will be broken
when you fall from your high office.

Dawn of a New Rainy Season

Dawn came as usual
but with a black face.
The vault of heaven
darkened in silence.
The thick morning breeze
draped with brown wear wept
when a roll of thunder
rolled across the dark sky
heralding new weather,
the season of wetness
when the rain drums loudest.

Wroth claps of thunder
aflame with flurry
woke the neighbourhood.
Lightning flashed and flashed,
struck seven lean goats,
hit a few houses
and split a lone palm tree.
At the drop of a hat
the overburdened sky
emptied its large bladder
on the bald head of earth.

It rained and rained hard,
laughing to scorn drought
drowning side by side
dust under a cloud.
No soul stepped outside
to toast with the rain

or deck it with laurels.
In time the earth will swell
with motherly fine airs
and give birth to new life.

The rain petered out
three hours to twilight.
I ventured outside
as nightfall crawled in.
A headless building
with children wet through
and a lifeless figure
baited my attention.
I lingered for a while
to brood over this time,
the new rainy season.

Braving the Rainy Season

This rainy season
with its watery mouth
and freezing fingers
makes water everywhere.

Plains put on green garments
valleys fill with water
hills smile in their new robes
and the air caresses
newly sprung hibiscus.
The once sore earth softened
welcomes every good seed.

This rainy season
with its clammy hands
and gushing nozzles
weeps in every quarter.

Frogs croak special numbers
crickets shatter the air
with shrills of untamed glee
when night loosens their tongues.
Nightjars come together
in the darkness dancing
to keep in step with time.

This rainy season
stoops to no man's cry
when lightning strikes hope.
Floods crack open graves,

flood the lands of peasants
and sometimes wipe them out.
My mind this wet season
eats its godlike heart out
for days to think up words
that console drooping hearts
and paint the landscape bright.
I feel this year's wetness
deep in my brittle bones.

This rainy season
with its storming storms
and slippery slopes
so many and muddy
may not put loud laughter
in the mouths of farmers.
The flowers will flourish
and lovers will wear out
in the cold their passion.
Fireflies will come out
longing to pierce darkness.
I need to wrap myself
to brave the storms this year.

Carry Me Away

Lead me fair memory
through these cloudless moments
to where my afterbirth,
my umbilical cord
and my square ancestors
decked in redress repose.

Wheel me scrupulous mind
round the edges of doubt
towards my treeless realm
to feel the arms of care,
the warmth of belonging
around my heart at sea.

Carry me gentle memory
away from these dry surroundings
to where green belts and igneous rocks,
birds and animals breathe in peace,
where grasshoppers, crickets, gadflies,
butterflies, praying mantis, frogs
and soldier ants congregate
to drink the water of freedom.

Carry me microscopic mind
to the margins of Yemenong
the river struggling to resist
the heat and the toxic gases,
the load of rubbish, the miasma

killing streams, lakes ,ponds and rivers.
I want to be certain fair mind
that you will not uncover me.

Before We Ceased To Be

Remember my beloved
the hills from which we come,
the streams from which we drank
before we were burdened
with smells that choke the mind.
Remember my beloved
the rocks from which we come,
the earth that suckled us
before we ceased to be
architects of our fate.

Leave me a place my beloved
on the cushion of your heart
where I can lie down and rest
when tongues yellowed from decay
drive me crazy with their lies.
Our dignity may be gone
and mould may creep up our walls
but I know your heart and mine
framed like identical twins
would plunder treason one day.

If I cannot have what I want
except by kissing bloke arses
from the bowels of the forest,
the rolling hills from which I come
will heartily welcome me back.
The rocks too will leave me a place
in the middle of the palace
where I can grow what I want

and beat the drums of liberty
without pythons, without monsters.

Before we ceased to be anything
we could ride on the wings of a storm.
Not knowing greed we did not sow greed.
The fights we had were not as deadly
as the eggs of a poisonous snake.
We knew we were either sand or dust
waiting to be blown away by time.
We spent much time searching between cracks
scorpions and other poisonous bugs
to keep our offspring from dying young.

Deep In The Grasslands

Where hills seem to kiss
and goats mate like dogs
deep in the grasslands
in the far north-west region
lies my umbilical cord,
the link with my ancestors.

The coffee eyes of the earth
and the dry whispering wind
make my people lose their nerves.
I seek to remake history
on the ashes of gone stars
ready to drop any time.

There is nothing wrong
writing poems with wings
and dancing naked
in the firm grip of Esu
where memory takes flight
on the wings of belonging.

The setting sun sometimes mocks
men trembling like windblown reeds
drunk like early morning bees.
I seek with the troubled world
to tend without stop stung hearts
before the earth swallows me.

Where hills butterfly
and swallows make love
between sky and earth
deep deep down in my village
dozes my belly button
the bridge with my kith and kin.

Stretches of Green

Stretches of green here and there
sometimes very very thick
sometimes surprisingly sparse.
Bayreuth and Emden have them
and the people worship them.
They seem to relieve their pain
and see tomorrow in them.
Germany cherishes them.

Trees and grass are a treasure
just as dogs and cats win love.
The moisture under the trees
and the wind, the cooling wind
blows hope into their homesteads.
Their hearts are tied to the trees
entangled as it would seem
in the gauzy threads of self.
Germany cultivates green.

I caught my stark-naked self
sulking alone in the trees
thinking about Cameroon
my blessed bizarre fatherland
where people in love with cash
take life from our trees instead.
When every tree must have been felled
and ferried to Europe for gold,
the desert alive like a heart
will make love with us on the sand.

Morning Kiss

A bee kissed my ear
early one morning
and flew away gay.
I stared at it lame
and felt rage well up
inside me like rain
though I felt no pain.

It landed on a flower
swaying in the morning breeze,
sang a sweet seductive song
before sucking her rounded breasts.
Satisfied,it sang one more time
before taking off in grand style.
It's joy left a wound in my heart
as I turned round to face the day.

I have longed to fly away
from the incessant quarrels
and the lies of politicians
turning the heads of my people.
I have longed to be like a bee,
like my early morning caller
sucking the sweet breasts of nature
to gather more sting by the day
for robbers and politicians.

I have longed to fly away
from self to kiss weary hearts
asleep in trash cans with worms

and make them relive the fragrance
and the happy life that was theirs
before their flowers were destroyed.
I have longed to suck the nectar
from flowers to give birth to joy.
The politician fears my dream
dancing in the midst of his pawns.

Fruitful Visit

With elegance and care
in the heart of blooms bright
a butterfly in blue
alights on a rose spent
having spent time waiting
for a visit worthwhile.

A protracted caress
ruptures the pollen bag
scattering the powder.
The rose over the moon
opens up in a flash
kissing the butterfly
a thousand and one times
mindless of the pollen
borne by the flirting wind
to beget new roses.

Sated,the butterfly
blind drunk with enjoyment
takes wing to a new bloom
forget-me-not in bud.
Tiny showers of rain
force it to retire.

Nobody gives a damn
to the many roses
and the forget-me-not
flowers blooming in pain.
I stand with you fair blooms

to water your petals
bruised when ravenous guests
jump into your light beds.
Never send bees away
nor moths nor butterflies.

Scaly Skunk

On the left of my workshop
stands a wooden whitewashed wall
whose undressed maggoty top
seduces little reptiles.
At the crack of dawn mainly
a fair fully-fledged lizard
leaves the ground for the rank top
to snatch at a bite to eat
before the sun bakes the place.

Curiosity goaded me
into heeding my instincts.
I am not a lizard though.
I went outside eyes sharpened
not to shoot the scaly skunk,
not to capture it either
nor show my superior size,
not for sway did I come out
but to penetrate the brute.

Leaning against a pear tree
barren since it came to be
I watched the cold-blooded beast
run like the wind to the wall.
It nodded a good few times
and started to climb with glee
the treen wall to its side dish.
Curiosity lost its voice
and I lapsed into thought.

The earth will kiss both of us
when our day of leaving lights
and the lights of life glow dim.
I spent the rest of the time
in a misty dream groaning
as the lizard broke its fast
on maggots and bluebottles.
Out of my windowless dream
I tiptoed into my shack.

The Gecko and the Spider

I saw a grey gecko
gazing at a spider
rounding off its new web
on a colourless wall.
It had been crocheting
for three days and three nights
dreaming of a big catch
in the hub of dryness
to blot out its want pangs.

Suddenly like lightning
the gecko, tail lifted,
eyes bulging with hunger
sprang into wild action,
seized the off guard creature
and gobbled it choking,
blind to its own frailty.
A spell of weird silence
left a blot in my heart.

Dark with melancholy
in the dark of this world,
I felt the claws of hate
deep hate for predators
dig deep into my breast.
I picked up an old broom
but before I raised it
the filthy animal
blot in my landscape fled.

Fury with frustration
forced my me into bed
but I could not find sleep.
The whisper of dry winds
in the trees at death's door
begging to quench their thirst
captured my attention.
I did not sleep that night
and my landscape brooded.

When under my own steam
I think of the gecko
and the spider devoured,
my eyes quicken with grief.
Tears pour for my country,
my bent rainbow nation,
the spider working hard
to be swallowed by greed
the blot on my landscape.

Green with Envy

Rabbits of every hue
from every neighbourhood
love to make love and breed
in this secluded place
when the day is balmy
and beetles groan on heat
where the dust breathes slowly.
I love the placement too
when it is cool and windy
and butterflies flap their wings
dressed in arresting colours.

Bush babies trust the wild
and bow when lightning strikes.
They shun where noise rises
like waves in the ocean
to break their line of thought
and kill them for food.
I too hate fruitless noise
when I am in a shade
contemplating ants at work,
watching how flies on dead mice
fight to eat before sunset.

With my hand on my breast
and my mind in your land
I celebrate your drive
never to kill for sport
nor play false for trophies.
You wear no dark glasses

to head off detection
when nature becomes wild
and the earth gathers courage
to face with tenacity
the strokes of man's treachery.

I envy you creatures
loose in your nakedness.
When the moon smiles you smile
whereas man looks daggers
in the dark of his heart
planning to cut my throat.
Your love pierces the night
dancing against the storm
brewing in the horizon.
I envy you simple friends
free to do what pleases you.

Another Night

The stars are dim tonight
for any reflection.
The moon is faint and light
for fun wine and roses.
The wind flaps its strong wings,
peels off and sweeps my hat
into a garbage can
as soon as I step outside
to clear my head heart and soul
before the bug of railing
against rats comes over me.
Only justice can kill it.

The wind is howling still
stealing a march on owls
gathered to map out death.
Light fingers, state agents
and their mainstay their heads
gather too in their den
to shape their next action.
These creative accountants
plunder with impunity
funds from the national purse.
Kindle a light brainboxes
in the darkness of your psyches
before the itch of kicking
against marauding rulers
comes over the silent lot
lost after voting for change.
Only justice can stop them.

Storm on, storm on wild wind
for darkness to tremble.
Storm harder, storm a gale,
a force nine gale tonight.
I need a new workshop
in the neck of the woods
near a fast flowing stream
bordering reality and sham.
We need a new direction
to strike a chord inside us
in the darkness of our thoughts
before the wind not so slack
as man's compromising breast
spurs me into whipping wimps.
I must find something solid,
something indestructible
something I can pivot on
when the wind like a mad bull
clears the deck for unused brooms.
Only justice can save us.

The Darkness inside Kills

The darkness outside
flirting with wind
not for distinction
but for diversion
does not freeze my blood.
It is established.

The darkness inside
conversing with you
not for formation
but for projection
makes my blood run cold.
It has iron teeth.

It is your heart I desire
not your testimonials nor look,
not your background nor scholarship
but passion that fires the blood.
You may not be able my friend
to chew and swallow my concepts.
You can keep open house for them
but do not turn their stomachs please
nor send them away in the buff.
It disconcerts me deep inside.

The darkness outside does not kill.
It is the darkness in your heart,
the slings and arrows in your eyes
and ignorance your bosom friend
that nip in the bud the freedom
to laugh with the waves of the sea.

I have seen from my atelier
the fiesta of green fresh flowers
in the fields of my fatherland.
It warms the cockles of my heart.

My Rose Is Still Cute

I can call to mind
the very last time
I laughed like the moon.
It was in my room
thirty-three years back.
Happy as a lark
I burst out laughing
watching a rare rose
lovely to behold
on my bed of wool.

Though a little grey
drained by the weather
the rose is still cute.
My rose still smells nice
in spite of the mud
and the muck outside.
I pray with my heart
it does not wither
ahead of the time
determined by God.

I see my spouse in the rose
my itch for her round her neck.
I wish she could put it on
long without bells and whistles.
I see my bloom in the kids
born and raised in the garden
where God alone points the way
and nature knuckles under.

I wish we could touch your hearts
and fell the foul trees in them.

A Tree of Even Temper

A tree of even temper
germinated in my heart
when I was still unseasoned
in the blossom-time of life.
It has grown big and mature
just as I am full of years.
It has borne a lot of fruit
and still bears succulent fruits
in the wet and the dry seasons.
The unfledged as well as the old
kill their hunger day after day
plucking fleshy fruits from the tree.

I can no longer withstand
the stones thrown at me daily.
My age can no longer bear
the weight of your gluttony.
If your heart has ever felt
the teeth of repudiation
you will never purse your lips
when injustice flogs a man
for his mind and integrity.
I feel the pressure to adapt
closing in rapidly on me
like the stench from an open grave.

I cannot betray my likes
even when the cracks of whips
descend on my aged sore back.
I cannot betray my flesh

even when I am dying.
Chieftains have become heartless
yet some of my kind praise them,
doting on them day by day.
They crush anyone on their way
and are as greedy as the grave.
I see them in the dish of worms
seasoned with wrath and revulsion.

Let Me Plough with You

If any virtue
still resides in you
let me sit down here
in this sumptuous room
where your heart slumbers.
Let me breathe the air
absent where I live
as dry as the dust
blot on my landscape.

The absence of rot
and the smell of mice
diminish the strain
and the burning shame
in my inmost soul.
This place consoles me
though my people rust
nailed shut in squabbles
blot on our landscape.

If anything worthy
can still come out of you
let me in my grey age
plough together with you
to have a great harvest.
Let me have a hand in
the shaping of your mind
to bring you back to us
before blot blows you out.

My threescore years and three
have taught me how to live
in thatched huts with scorpions
and in suites with villains
prepared to slash your throat
to rise to hold the reins.
I can freely school you
in the art of backlash
to save you from collapse.

We can rule the roost too
and out-Herod Herod
to heal our diseased land
and get rid of toadies.
Our foes shoot from ambush
eager to take our lives
to keep mangling the land.
I see you in new robes
plucking the eyes of blot.

Make Melody

Make melody my heart
in the mood of the moon.
Make melody my soul
in the heart of my heart
not to be eye-catching
but to be soul-searching
in this uncouth wasteland.

Make music my muscles
in the chest of falsehood.
Make music my sinews
in the womb of this wild
not to cut a figure
but to stir consciences
blunted in this desert.

Make melody my friend
in the presence of stars.
Make melody my blood
in the fields of my muse
not to swear by roguing
but to water morals
wilting in this dry land.

Make music son of Jah
in this prison holding.
Make music for the bound
kicking themselves in dung.
The ceaseless barbed laughter

of bloated birds of prey
runs a sword through their minds.

Make sweet-sounding music,
sound engaging music
for the health of the state.
This art of the Muses
blended with commitment
and love seasoned with truth
mends the state of the mind.

Make charming melody,
fresh rousing melody
for the soul of the state.
Sweet music cooked in wit
with a frenetic beat
can make an ass foxtrot
and the caged break cages.

Time to Clean

People who set out to live
to make life worthwhile living
in a world worn down by wars
but are at ease not speaking
in the face of oppression
the blot on our landscape
are not better than the dead.
Nature frowns on them daily.

I know that from time to time
in silence the heart does rave
thinking of the mosquitoes,
the distilleries of death
and the crippling breweries
blossoming in the country,
the forgotten toothless poor
and the drunken drones who run
over protesting voices
and drive over their bodies.

It is time to clean the land
and plant evergreen windbreaks
to deal deforestation
disciples a deadly blow
for stars not yet come to light
to bring to light the bright green
face of a brutalised land
and a corrupted landscape.

It is time to clean the mess

and purge the land of bent brains
to raise a statue of green
where ecologists grow pale
smeared with wet droppings and sweat.
Factories churn out lethal smoke,
my flesh crawls with wireworms
in the height of pollution.
I cannot have a field day
in the backyard of slovens.

Printed in the United States
By Bookmasters